TRAV...
THE...

Traverse Theatre Company
The Trestle at Pope Lick Creek
by Naomi Wallace

cast in order of appearance

Dalton Chance	Ian Skewis
Pace Creagan	Julia Dalkin
Chas Weaver	Eric Barlow
Gin Chance	Pauline Knowles
Dray Chance	Iain Macrae

director	Philip Howard
designer	Fiona Watt
lighting designer	Renny Robertson
composer	Gavin Marwick
voice & dialect coach	Ros Steen
assistant director	Helen-Marie O'Malley
stage manager	Gavin Harding
deputy stage manager	Victoria Paulo
assistant stage manager	Brendan Graham
wardrobe supervisor	Lynn Ferguson
cutter	Jackie Holt
wardrobe assistant	Stephanie Thorburn
carpenter	Kris Whitehead

Supported by the **Peggy Ramsay Foundation**

**The Trestle at Pope Lick Creek was first performed
at the Humana Festival, Louisville
Friday 13 March 1998**

**First performance of this production at the Traverse Theatre
Friday 16 February 2001**

TRAVERSE THEATRE

One of the most important theatres in Britain The Observer

Edinburgh's **Traverse Theatre** is Scotland's new writing theatre, with a 37 year record of excellence. With quality, award-winning productions and programming, the Traverse receives accolades at home and abroad from audiences and critics alike.

The Traverse has an unrivalled reputation for producing contemporary theatre of the highest quality, invention and energy, commissioning and supporting writers from Scotland and around the world and facilitating numerous script development workshops, rehearsed readings and public writing workshops. The Traverse aims to produce several major new theatre productions plus a Scottish touring production each year. It is unique in Scotland in its exclusive dedication to new writing, providing the infrastructure, professional support and expertise to ensure the development of a sustainable and relevant theatre culture for Scotland and the UK.

Traverse Theatre Company productions have been seen worldwide including London, Toronto, Budapest and New York. Recent touring successes in Scotland include PERFECT DAYS by Liz Lochhead, PASSING PLACES by Stephen Greenhorn, HIGHLAND SHORTS, HERITAGE by Nicola McCartney and LAZYBED by Iain Crichton Smith. PERFECT DAYS also played the Vaudeville Theatre in London's West End in 1999. In 2000 the Traverse co-produced Michel Tremblay's SOLEMN MASS FOR A FULL MOON IN SUMMER with London's Barbican Centre, with performances in both Edinburgh and London, and two world premieres as part of the Edinburgh Festival Fringe: SHETLAND SAGA by Sue Glover and ABANDONMENT by Kate Atkinson. AMONG UNBROKEN HEARTS by Henry Adam will be seen in April 2001 at The Bush Theatre, London, following its successful run at the Traverse and subsequent tour of Scotland.

The Traverse can be relied upon to produce more good-quality new plays than any other Fringe venue
Daily Telegraph

During the Edinburgh Festival the Traverse is one of the most important venues with world class premieres playing daily in the two theatre spaces. The Traverse regularly wins awards at the Edinburgh Festival Fringe, including recent *Scotsman Fringe Firsts* for Traverse productions KILL THE OLD TORTURE THEIR YOUNG by David Harrower and PERFECT DAYS by Liz Lochhead.

An essential element of the Traverse Company's activities takes place within the educational sector, concentrating on the process of playwriting for young people. The Traverse flagship education project CLASS ACT offers young people in schools the opportunity to work with theatre professionals and see their work performed on the Traverse stage. In addition the Traverse runs Young Writers groups for 15 - 25 year olds and Shining Souls, a writers group for people aged 55+. All groups are led by professional playwrights.

NAOMI WALLACE

Naomi was born in Kentucky. She graduated from the University of Iowa in 1993. Her first production for the stage THE WAR BOYS at London's Finborough Theatre in 1993 was followed by IN THE FIELDS OF ACELDAMA and her children's play THE GIRL WHO FELL THROUGH A HOLE IN HER JUMPER (co-written with Bruce McLeod) which were produced in the London New Play Festival in 1993 and 1994 respectively. Naomi also co-wrote IN THE SWEAT with Bruce McLeod for the National Theatre's education department for the 1997 BT/National Connections.

Naomi's London West End debut was in 1997 with her stage adaptation of William Wharton's classic novel BIRDY which followed successful runs at London's Lyric Theatre, Hammersmith and the Drum Theatre, Plymouth in 1996. Naomi's New York debut took place four days later at the Joseph Papp Public Theatre in March 1997 with ONE FLEA SPARE, winning a prestigious Obie Award. The play was first produced in 1995 at the Bush Theatre, London. IN THE HEART OF AMERICA premiered at the Bush Theatre, London in 1994. IN THE HEART OF AMERICA and ONE FLEA SPARE both won the Susan Smith Blackburn Prize, making Naomi the only writer ever to have won this award twice.

Naomi's Mobil Playwriting Competition prize-winning play SLAUGHTER CITY received its World Premiere by the RSC in January 1996 and its US Premier shortly afterwards by The American Repertory Theatre. THE TRESTLE AT POPE LICK CREEK premiered at the 1998 Humana Festival, Louisville and opened at New York Theatre Workshop in June 1999.

In 1999 she was awarded the MacArthur Foundation Genius Grant.

Naomi's first feature film LAWN DOGS opened in the UK at the London Film Festival in November 1997, having won the Best Screenplay award at the Sitges Festival in Spain. Produced by Duncan Kenworthy (Four Weddings And A Funeral) and directed by John Duigan, LAWN DOGS was made just five months after Kenworthy optioned the "spec" script. Her second feature ONE FLEA SPARE (adapted by her with Bruce McLeod from Naomi's play) has been commissioned by Kenworthy for DNA. She has adapted, with Bruce McLeod, Carolyn Haines's novel TOUCHED as a feature for Dogstar, now with David Parfitt's Trademark Films. Her screenplay THE WAR BOYS (adapted from her play with Bruce McLeod) will be shot this spring in San Diego.

Naomi's poetry has been published on both sides of the Atlantic. She has won the National Poetry Prize in America and in 1995 her first poetry collection TO DANCE A STONY FIELD was published in the UK by Peterloo Poets.

BIOGRAPHIES

Eric Barlow *(Chas)*: Trained: Queen Margaret College, Edinburgh. For the Traverse: SHETLAND SAGA, THE SPECULATOR, HERITAGE, THE ARCHITECT. Other theatre includes: RUG COMES TO SHUV (Theatre Gerrard Phillipe, Paris); PORTRAIT OF A WOMAN, THE SUICIDE (Communicado); MACBETH, PETER PAN, THREE SISTERS, THE SHAUGHRAUN, MOTHER COURAGE, HAMLET, MUCH ADO ABOUT NOTHING, THE MERCHANT OF VENICE, THE CAUCASIAN CHALK CIRCLE, WAITING FOR GODOT, OUR COUNTRY'S GOOD, HANSEL AND GRETEL, SLEEPING BEAUTY, THE TAMING OF THE SHREW, BEAUTY AND THE BEAST, MERLIN THE MAGNIFICENT, THE PRINCESS AND THE GOBLIN, ARSENIC AND OLD LACE, MERLIN - SEARCH FOR THE GRAIL, MIRANDOLINA (Royal Lyceum); ROMEO AND JULIET, MACBETH, LOVE BUT HER (Brunton), THE SALT WOUND (7:84), THE WISHING TREE (Wiseguise), THE HARP AND THE VIOLET, THE PRINCESS AND THE GOBLIN (Dundee Rep); THE CHIC MURRAY STORY (Pavilion). Film includes: ORPHANS (Antonine), MY LIFE SO FAR (Miramax), THE INITIATION, HARD NUT - A LOVE STORY (Ideal World). Television includes: THE YOUNG PERSON'S GUIDE TO BECOMING A ROCK STAR (Channel 4), MURDER ROOMS - THE DARK BEGINNINGS OF SHERLOCK HOLMES, McCALLUM, TAGGART, DR FINDLAY (STV), RAB C NESBITT (BBC). Radio includes: SWANSONG, HYDRO, TALL DROLL, AFTER ICARUS.

Julia Dalkin *(Pace)*: Trained: RSAMD. Theatre includes: EGIL, SON OF THE NIGHT WOLF (Grey Coast Theatre); ALADDIN (Cumbernauld Theatre); SPEED THE PLOW (Arches). Film and television includes: THE GLASS, FOUR MORE HOURS, LIFE SUPPORT, WING AND A PRAYER, INSPECTOR MORSE. Radio includes: DR WHO: PHANTASMAGORIA, PRAVDA STREET.

Philip Howard (director): Philip trained at the Royal Court Theatre, London, on the Regional Theatre Young Director Scheme from 1988-90. He was Associate Director at the Traverse from 1993-96, and has been Artistic Director since 1996. Productions for the Traverse include: LOOSE ENDS, BROTHERS OF THUNDER, EUROPE, KNIVES IN HENS (also The Bush Theatre), THE ARCHITECT, FAITH HEALER, WORMWOOD, LAZYBED, THE CHIC NERDS, KILL THE OLD TORTURE THEIR YOUNG, HERITAGE, THE SPECULATOR, HIGHLAND SHORTS, SOLEMN MASS FOR A FULL MOON IN SUMMER (with Ros Steen), SHETLAND SAGA. Philip's other theatre includes HIPPOLYTUS (Arts Theatre Cambridge), ENTERTAINING MR SLOANE (Royal, Northampton) and SOMETHING ABOUT US (Lyric Hammersmith Studio).

Pauline Knowles *(Gin)*: For the Traverse: SOLEMN MASS FOR A FULL MOON IN SUMMER, THE SPECULATOR, WIDOWS, THE COLLECTION, MARISOL, KNIVES IN HENS (also The Bush Theatre). Other theatre includes: VASSA (Almeida); KING LEAR, PETER PAN (Theatre Babel); OTHELLO (TAG); SHINING SOULS (Old Vic); HEY, GOOD LOOKIN (Soho Theatre); MEN SHOULD WEEP, A SCOTS QUAIR (TAG); SWING HAMMER SWING (Citizens'); TWELFTH NIGHT (Royal Lyceum & Salisbury Theatre); CUTTIN' A RUG, SCHOOL FOR WIVES (Royal Lyceum); ANTIGONE, JUMP THE LIFE TO COME (7:84); OH WHAT A LOVELY WAR, SHARKS (Wildcat); VODKA AND DAISIES (Annexe); DON JUAN (Penname). Television includes: ACTING WITH RICHARD WILSON, STRATHBLAIR, JOHN BROWN'S BODY. Radio includes: FLOATING, SUBUTU PASSAGE, WANTIN' A HAND, LEAVE ME ALONE.

Iain Macrae *(Dray)*: Trained: Mountview Theatre School, London. For the Traverse: HIGHLAND SHORTS, HERITAGE, LAZYBED, PASSING PLACES. Other theatre includes: AN CLO MOR/THE BIG CLOTH (Theatre Highland); BEGIN AGAIN (KtC); PHAEDRA'S LOVE (Ghostown); THE AIPPLE TREE (Dràma na h-Alba); ATOMS OF DELIGHT (Eden Court Tour); SACRED GROUND (Watford Palace). Television includes: INTERROGATION OF A HIGHLAND LASS (BBC/Pelicula); FALACH FEAD (STV/Studio Alba); DWELLY (BBC/Eolas); MACHAIR (STV); RAN DAN, YEAR OF THE PRINCE, TUIG, DE-A-NIS? (BBC); CIORSTAIDH (STV/Grampian). Voice for numerous TV cartoons. Radio includes: 'P' DIVISION, DESPERATE JOURNEY, THE LETTER, NORTHERN TRAWL (BBC). Film includes: THE GIFT, MAIRI MHOR (BBC); AS AN EILEAN (C4); BEFORE WINTER WINDS, DATHAN (Geur Gheàrr/BBC).

Gavin Marwick (composer): Born Edinburgh. Founder member and composer with IRON HORSE, a contemporary traditional band which has toured over four continents and released five albums. Gavin also plays in a fiddle duo with Jonny Hardie (of OLD BLIND DOGS). For the Traverse: HIGHLAND SHORTS, HERITAGE, FAITH HEALER. For the BBC: THE GAME KEEPER. Discography: THE IRON HORSE, THRO WATER EARTH AND STONE, FIVE HANDS HIGH, VOICE OF THE LAND, DEMONS AND LOVERS (all for IRON HORSE), UP IN THE AIR, THE BLUE LAMP (with Jonny Hardie), THE WEIRD SET (with BURACH).

Renny Robertson (lighting designer): Renny is Chief Electrician at the Traverse Theatre. Lighting designs for the Traverse: FAITH HEALER, LAZYBED, WORMWOOD, THE CHIC NERDS, HERITAGE. He has created designs for several other companies, most recently Magnetic North and Lung Ha's.

Ian Skewis *(Dalton)*: Trained: RSAMD. For the Traverse: DANNY 306 + ME (4 EVER), Class Act 2000. Other theatre includes: MYTHS OF THE NEAR FUTURE, THE DROWNED SAINT (Tramway); OTHELLO (TAG); MERLIN THE MAGNIFICENT (Citizens'); BROADWAY BOUND, LEND ME A TENOR, PETER PAN (Perth Rep), MARTHA (Catherine Wheels Theatre Company); THE PRINCESS AND THE GOBLIN (MacRobert, Stirling); THE MAIDS (RSAMD). Film includes: BENT (Film Four). TV includes: HIGH ROAD (STV); G FORCE (BBC).

Ros Steen (voice & dialect coach): Trained: RSAMD. Ros co-directed SOLEMN MASS FOR A FULL MOON IN SUMMER for the Traverse. As voice/dialect coach for the Traverse: AMONG UNBROKEN HEARTS, SHETLAND SAGA, KING OF THE FIELDS, HIGHLAND SHORTS, FAMILY, HERITAGE, KILL THE OLD TORTURE THEIR YOUNG, THE CHIC NERDS, GRETA, LAZYBED, KNIVES IN HENS, PASSING PLACES, BONDAGERS, ROAD TO NIRVANA, SHARP SHORTS, MARISOL, GRACE IN AMERI-CA, BROTHERS OF THUNDER. Other theatre includes: FUNHOUSE, OLEANNA, SUMMIT CONFERENCE, KRAPP'S LAST TAPE, THE DYING GAUL, CONVERSATION WITH A CUPBOARD MAN, EVA PERON, LONG DAY'S JOURNEY INTO NIGHT, (Citizens'); A.D. (Raindog); PLAYBOY OF THE WESTERN WORLD, A MIDSUMMER NIGHT'S DREAM (Dundee Rep); SEA URCHINS (Tron & Dundee Rep); HOME, TRANSATLANTIC, THE HANGING TREE, LAUNDRY and ENTERTAINING ANGELS (LookOut); ODYSSEUS THUMP (West Yorkshire Playhouse); BEUL NAM BREUG (Tosg Theatar Gaidhlig); TRAVELS WITH MY AUNT, THE PRICE (Brunton); TRAINSPOTTING (G & J Productions); HOW TO SAY GOODBYE, BABYCAKES (Clyde Unity); ABIGAIL'S PARTY (Perth Rep); LOVERS, PYGMALION, OUR COUN-TRY'S GOOD (Royal Lyceum); SUNSET SONG (TAG). Film includes: GREGORY'S TWO GIRLS, STELLA DOES TRICKS, STAND AND DELIVER. Television includes: 2000 ACRES OF SKY, MONARCH OF THE GLEN, HAMISH MACBETH, LOOKING AFTER JOJO, ST ANTHONY'S DAY OFF, CHANGING STEP.

Fiona Watt (designer): Trained: Motley (Almeida). Awarded Arts Council of England Resident Design Bursary 1996 (Wolsey, Ipswich). For the Traverse: HIGHLAND SHORTS, HERITAGE. Other theatre includes: THE BOOK OF MIRACLES (Nottingham Roundabout); SANCTUARY (Yorkshire Women); JULIUS CAESAR (TAG), OUTWARD BOUND, LOVE BITES (Palace Theatre, Watford); A WALK ON LAKE ERIE (Finborough); GRACE IN AMERICA (Old Red Lion). Opera: LA PIETRA DEL PARAGONE (RSAMD). Film: NITRATE WON'T WAIT (First Reels). Exhibition: TIME & SPACE (RCA, London) and THEATRE DESIGN at the Tron as part of the UK City of Architecture & Design.

**For generous help on THE TRESTLE AT POPE LICK CREEK
the Traverse thanks:**

LEVER BROTHERS for wardrobe care

Sets, props and costumes for THE TRESTLE AT POPE LICK CREEK
created by Traverse Workshops *(funded by the National Lottery)*

THE SCOTTISH ARTS COUNCIL
National Lottery Fund

scenic artists Monique Jones, Tom Aldridge

production photography Kevin Low
print photography Euan Myles

SPONSORSHIP

Sponsorship income enables the Traverse to commission and produce
new plays and offer audiences a diverse and exciting
programme of events throughout the year.
**We would like to thank the following companies for their support
throughout the year:**

CORPORATE ASSOCIATE SCHEME

LEVEL ONE
Sunday Herald
Balfour Beatty
Scottish Life the PENSION company
United Distillers & Vintners
Amanda Howard Associates

LEVEL TWO
Laurence Smith -
Wine Merchants
Willis Corroon Scotland Ltd
Wired Nomad

LEVEL THREE
Alistir Tait FGA
Antiques & Fine Jewellery
Nicholas Groves Raines –
Architects
KPMG
Scottish Post Office Board

BANK OF SCOTLAND

E S P C

B B C Scotland

artism

With thanks to
Navy Blue Design, print designers for the Traverse,
and Stewarts Colour Print
Arts & Business for management and mentoring services
Purchase of the Traverse Box Office, computer network and technical and
training equipment has been made possible with money from
The Scottish Arts Council National Lottery Fund.

THE SCOTTISH ARTS COUNCIL
National Lottery Fund

The Traverse Theatre's work would not be possible without the support of

THE SCOTTISH ARTS COUNCIL   ◆EDINBVRGH◆
THE CITY OF EDINBURGH COUNCIL

**The Traverse receives financial assistance for its educational and
development work from**
John Lewis Partnership, Peggy Ramsay Foundation, Binks Trust, The Yapp
Charitable Trusts, The Bulldog Prinsep Theatrical Trust, Calouste Gulbenkian
Foundation, Gannochy Trust, The Garfield Weston Foundation, The Paul Hamlyn
Foundation, JSP Pollitzer Charitable Trust, The Hope Trust, Steel Trust, Craignish
Trust, esmee Fairbairn Trust, Lindsay's Charitable Trust.

Charity No. SC002368

viii

TRAVERSE THEATRE - THE COMPANY

Jeremy Adderley	Bar Café Manager
Maria Bechaalani	Deputy Electrician
David Connell	Finance Manager
Pauline Diamond	Literary Assistant
Jude Durnan	Deputy Box Office Manager
Eric Dickinson	Kitchen Assistant
John Dyer	Head Chef
Lynn Ferguson	Wardrobe Supervisor
Michael Fraser	Theatre Manager
David Freeburn	Box Office Manager
Duncan Gray	Assistant Electrician
Mike Griffiths	Production Manager
Jayne Gross	Development Manager
Kellie Harris	Second Chef
David Henderson	Bar Café Attendant
Philip Howard	Artistic Director
Louise Ironside	SAC Resident Playwright
Mark Leese	Design Associate
Nicola Levitan	Asst Bar Café Manager
Catherine MacNeil	Administrator
Jan McTaggart	Virtual Traverse Project Officer
Lucy Mason	Administrative Producer
Katherine Mendelsohn	International Literary Associate
Kate Nelson	Monday Lizard Co-ordinator
Duncan Nicoll	Deputy Bar Café Manager
Paul Nowak	Box Office Assistant
Matthew Pichel-Juan	Bar Café Supervisor
Pauleen Rafferty	Finance & Personnel Assistant
Cathie Robertson	Administrative Assistant
Renny Robertson	Chief Electrician
Hannah Rye	Literary Development Officer
Zoe Squair	Front of House Manager
Fiona Sturgeon	Marketing Manager
John Tiffany	Literary Director
Jenni Wardle	Press & Development Officer
Brian Weller	Deputy Production Manager

Also working for the Traverse: Louise Anderson, Karen Aspen, Paul Axford, Nancy Birch, Simon Breslaw, Anna Copland, Jamie Costello, Ben Ewart-Dean, Simon Flisher, Vikki Graves, Linda Gunn, Maria Hodson, Nathan Huxtable, David Inverarity, Emilie Janiaud, Chris Jones, Tamsin Le Marie, Amy Liptrot, Sophie Logan, Kevin McCune, Donna McGlynn, Callum McIntosh, Alison McLeod, Clare Padgett, Rowan Paton-Risby, Gavin Rae, Dominic Rafferty, Naomi Schwock, Sara Shiel, Alison Smith, Kate Stone, Alistair Stott, Alexandra Turnbull

TRAVERSE THEATRE BOARD OF DIRECTORS
Stuart Hepburn (Chair), **Kate Atkinson, Steven Cotton, Geraldine Gammell, Lesley Riddoch, Stuart Murray** (Company Secretary)

Naomi Wallace
The Trestle at Pope Lick Creek

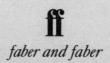

faber and faber

Published in 2001
by Faber and Faber Limited
3 Queen Square, London WC1N 3AU

Typeset by Country Setting, Kingsdown, Kent CT14 8ES
Printed in England by Mackays of Chatham plc, Chatham, Kent

A CIP record for this book
is available from the British Library

ISBN 0-571-21075-9

2 4 6 8 10 9 7 5 3 1

For my friend Mark Landrum,
who made the crossing,
and for those who didn't

And for Marianne Macy,
who was there

Nothing in the world is single

Percy Bysshe Shelley

Characters

Pace Creagan
A girl, seventeen years old

Dalton Chance
A boy, fifteen years old

Gin Chance
Dalton's mother, forty-one years old

Dray Chance
Dalton's father, a few years Gin's senior

Chas Weaver
A jailer, Brett's father, early fifties

Time
1936

Place
A town outside a city. Somewhere in the United States

Set
Should be minimal and not 'realistic'

Note
Accents of the characters should be as 'neutral'
as possible – from 'somewhere' in the US

Prologue

Darkness. Then we see Dalton sitting upstage, in a corner. His back is all we see. Beside him is a small candle. From the light of the candle, Dalton makes hand shadows. We can see the shadows but we cannot discern what they are.

Dalton This is a. Horse. (*He makes another hand shadow.*) This is a swan. No. Not a swan, shit. A falcon. Yeah. A falcon. No. There's no claw. It's a duck. (*He makes another hand shadow.*) Now it's a turtle. There's the shell. But hell. It could be a fish. With a fin. (*He makes another hand shadow.*)

Pace appears. She is there but not there. Standing behind Dalton.

Pace That's not a fish, Dalton Chance. You should know better. That's a bird. A pigeon. The kind that lives under the trestle.

Dalton slowly turns and peers into the darkness. He doesn't see Pace, though she is visible to us. He calls softly.

Dalton Creagan? Pace Creagan? Is that you? (*Dalton stands up. He cries out to her.*) You go to hell, Pace Creagan!

Pace tips the candle over and there is darkness.

Act One

SCENE ONE

Months earlier, two youths, Pace and Dalton, run to meet under the trestle at Pope Lick Creek. Pace gets there ahead of Dalton. They have been running and are both out of breath.

Dalton You had a head start!

Pace Nah. You haven't got any lungs in that puny chest of yours. Listen to you rattle.

Dalton I'm not rattlin'.

Pace Yeah you are. What've you got in there? A handful of nails.

Dalton Twisted my ankle.

Pace Yeah, yeah.

Dalton So this is it, huh?

They look up above them.

Pace Yep.

Dalton It's not that high up.

Pace Almost a hundred feet. From the creek up.

Dalton Some creek. There's no water: it's dry.

Pace Don't care; can't swim anyway. What time is it?

Dalton Coming up to seven.

Pace Exact time.

Dalton (*guessing*) Six forty-one.

Pace She comes through at seven-ten. Sometimes seven-twelve. Sometimes she'll come on at seven-nine for ten days straight and then bang, she's off three minutes. She's never exact; you can't trust her. That's what I like.

Dalton How many times have you done it?

Pace Twice. Once with Jeff Farley. Once alone.

Dalton You're lyin'. Jeff Farley never ran it.

Pace Nope. Never did. Tied his shoes on real tight, took two deep breaths, said, 'I'm ready when you are.' And then he heard that whistle. Aren't a lot of people can hear that whistle.

Dalton So you didn't do it twice.

Pace I would of but he turned tail and ran.

Dalton So how many times then? Just once?

Pace Once. And that's once more than you.

Dalton Yeah. Who was witness?

Pace No one here to see me.

Dalton You're lying.

Pace Whatever you say.

Dalton Did you run it or not?

Pace Sure. Once.

Dalton How come I don't believe you?

Pace Me and you, we'll have witnesses. Philip, Lester and Elizabeth Landrum will be here at seven-o-five.

Dalton No. No way. You said just you and me as witness.

Pace If you get scared and run, who's to say you won't lie and say I chickened too?

Dalton You said just you and me.

Pace It'll be just you and me. Up there. Down here in the creek bed we'll have the three stooges watching us. Keeping tabs. Taking notes. And you can be sure they'll check our pants when we're done and see who's shit.

Dalton You know. You don't talk like a girl. Should.

Pace (*meaning it*) Thanks.

Dalton But you look like one. So I guess you are.

Pace Want me to prove it?

Dalton No.

Pace How old are you?

Dalton Sixteen. In a couple of months.

Pace (*nears him*) Well, well. Almost a man. (*Pushes him backwards, but not too hard.*) Listen to me, Dalton Chance, two years my junior, and shut up. Here's what we're going to do.

Dalton Just spell it out for me. Once and clear.

Pace OK. She's pulling eight cars at seventy tons apiece at eighty-five. Not a big one, as far as they go. But big enough. The engine herself's one hundred and fifty-three tons. And not cotton, kid. Just cold, lip-smackin' steel. Imagine a kiss like that. Just imagine it.

Dalton How do you know what the train weighs?

Pace I looked her up. The year, the weight, the speed.

Dalton So you can read.

Pace Yeah, well. You and her are coming from opposite sides, right. You've got to time it exact 'cause you need to make it across before she hits the trestle. It's like playin' chicken with a car, only she's bigger and you're

13

not a car. The kick is once you get halfway across, don't turn back and try to outrun her. You lose time like that. Just face her and go.

Dalton So what if you know it's too close? You go for the side, right?

Pace There's no side.

Dalton Yes there is.

Pace There's no side. Look at it.

Dalton There's a side.

Pace What's the matter with you? Look at the tracks. Look at them. There are no sides.

Dalton So what do you do if you can't make it across before she starts over?

Pace You make the cross. That's all there is to it.

Dalton But what if you can't?

Pace Remember Brett Weaver?

Dalton That's different. He was drunk.

Pace He was not.

Dalton Yes he was. He was drunk.

Pace Say that again and I'll punch you.

Dalton The papers said he was drunk.

Pace Brett wasn't drunk. He was just slow.

Dalton Slow? He was on the track team.

Pace That night he was slow.

Dalton How do you know?

Pace I just know.

Dalton Well. I've had a look like I told you I would and I've decided: I'm not crossing.

Pace I knew it. I knew it.

Dalton Only a drunk or an idiot'd play that game. Not me.

Pace You got the heart of a rabbit. A dead rabbit. And now you owe me a buck.

Dalton No way. I never said for certain. I said maybe. And you said it was safe. You didn't say anything about there being no safety sides. You said it was a piece of cake.

Pace It is a piece of cake. If you time it right.

Dalton Forget it.

Pace You're breaking the deal. Pay me a buck right now or else.

Dalton I said no.

Pace (*calmly pulls a switchblade*) Then I'll hurt you.

Dalton Put that away. You're warped. That's what everyone says at school: Pace Creagan is warped.

Pace Then why'd you come up here with me? I'm not even your friend.

Dalton No. You're not my friend. My friends don't pull knives.

Pace You were starting to like me, though. I could tell. You said you'd run it with me.

Dalton I said I might. I thought it could be fun. Warped people can be fun sometimes.

Pace If you back down everyone will know.

Dalton I don't care. I don't have a fan club.

Pace Mary Ellen Berry is coming as witness too.

Dalton No she's not.

Pace I asked her to. And she knows you've got a fancy for her.

Dalton Big deal. I asked her out. She turned me down. End of story.

Pace She says you're too short.

Dalton I'm not short.

Pace I don't think she was talking height.

Dalton I'm leaving.

Pace Hey. I told her to give you a chance. She likes me. She listens to me. I told her you were going to cross the trestle with me. She said, 'Oh.' You know, like she was thinking things.

Dalton What things?

Pace You know. The way girls think things. One, two, three, about face. Change of season. Oh. She said, 'Oh' like she was about to change her mind.

Dalton Mary Ellen's popular. Why would she listen to you?

Pace (*shrugs*) I once told her to take off her clothes and she did.

Dalton And what does that mean?

Pace It means I can run faster than she can so she does what I tell her to do. And she'll be here tonight. She's coming to watch us cross.

Dalton You had a look at her? Naked? What's she like?

Pace I'd say she's on the menu. Front, back, and in reverse. You'd like her.

Dalton How would you know what I like? You're not good-looking.

Pace Yeah. But that's got nothing to do with trains.

Dalton So how close were you that time you crossed?

Pace I'd say I had 'bout eight seconds leeway.

Dalton Eight seconds. Sure.

Pace A kid could do it. Look. We won't do it tonight, okay. We'll work up to it. Tonight we'll just watch her pass. Take her measure. Check her steam. Make sure we got it down. Then when we're ready, we'll run her. It'll be a snap.

Dalton A snap. What if you trip?

Pace Brett tripped.

Dalton He was messed up. Even if he wasn't drunk. He used to hit himself in the face just for the fun of it. Brett was mental. He'd hit his own nose until it bled.

Pace Brett wasn't mental.

Dalton I saw Brett hit himself. I saw him do it.

Pace It's none of your business.

Dalton You were his girl.

Pace We were friends. I never kissed him. And you're gonna run the trestle. One of these days.

Dalton How come?

Pace 'Cause if you don't your life will turn out just like you think it will: quick, dirty and cold.

Dalton Hey. I might go to college when I graduate.

Pace You're not going to college. None of us are going to college.

Dalton I got the grades for it. That's what Mr Pearson says.

Pace And who's gonna pay for it? Look at your shoes.

Dalton Huh?

Pace Your shoes. If your mom's putting you in shoes like that then you aren't going to college. (*Beat.*) Come on. Let's go up and watch.

Dalton If I can't go to college, I'll just leave.

Pace Some things should stay in one place, Dalton Chance. You're probably one of them.

SCENE TWO

Dalton, some months later, in an empty cell. He looks older now, dishevelled. He just stares. And stares. At nothing. After some moments Chas, the jailer, enters. He seems friendly enough. Dalton doesn't acknowledge Chas' presence. Chas slips from one subject to the next, with hardly a pause.

Chas On break. Thought I'd sit it out with you. The other guy, across the hall. He's looking for grass in his cell. Thinks he's a moose. Could be some other herbivore but every now and then he lets out this call and it sounds close enough to a moose. Yesterday, a bug. Some kind of a beetle, I think, with huge claws. He used his arms like pinchers. Opening and closing them. Opening and closing. For hours. Wayne was leaning in to give him some grub and the next minute he caught Wayne around the neck. Almost choked him to death. While I was prying him off he's making this sound. A beetle sound,

I guess. Sort of like – (*Chas makes a 'beetle sound'.*)
Self-respect: gone. Was the manager of the Plate Glass
Company. A real Roosevelt man. Good to his men,
though he laid them off. Then his head went pop one day
and he started breaking up the plant. Glass everywhere.
Wrecked half the place. Even the WPA says close it
down. No one needs glass these days. Might want glass
but they don't need it. Mr Roosevelt, I say, want to buy
some glass? Them up high's got the money to want.
They don't have to go by need. What kind of a beetle
was it, you think? Big pinchers. Opening and closing.
How'd the visit go? I know your folks. Nice people.
Sorry to hear your daddy's still out of work. But who
isn't? Well, I'm not. I'm still here. Could be somewheres
else, like Spain shooting some whatyoucallem, but I
might get killed and then bein' here looks better. I had a
boy like you. You must have known my Brett at school.
Big fellow. Fast runner? Moose's easier to identify.
Distinctive. My break's about up. So what do you think,
kid? How many years do you think you'll get? Or will
they hang you? When they hang you the last thing you
hear is your own neck break. And if you got a thick neck
bone, a strong one, a young one, then it takes a while to
break clean through, sometimes hours, and all the while
you're dying you're hearing it snapping and crackling
and popping, just like a stick on the fire. So what do you
think?

Chas gets no response so he shrugs and leaves the cell.

Dalton A stag beetle. That's what kind it was.

SCENE THREE

Dalton is trying to get the shoes off his mother's feet after she's come home from work.

Dalton Yeah it does. I read it at the drugstore.

Gin Just leave it.

Dalton All your nerves're squashed up in the ball of your foot. Stop wiggling.

> *Dalton gets one of her shoes off. She relaxes now as he massages her feet.*

Gin How's the math going at school?

Dalton (*teasing*) You've got seven toes.

Gin Woman on the right of me, Barbara Hill, laid off Tuesday. Woman on my left, laid off today. Just waiting my turn.

Dalton You've been there forever. They need you.

Gin How is he?

Dalton Quiet.

Gin Yeah, quiet. (*Gin unwraps a small stack of plates. Looks at them. Then wraps them up again.*) It's getting harder to find the plates. Even the Salvation is running short. I don't want to use the ones my mother gave me. Might have to one of these days.

Dalton It'll be okay.

> *Dalton is finished with her feet. He begins to unpin her hair and then brush it. She lets him.*

Gin You got anything better to do with your afternoons than take care of an old mother when she comes home from work? You should be out with the boys. Yelling. Falling down. Doing fun things boys do. What do boys do for fun?

Dalton You know the trestle up at Pope Lick? Well, I was with a girl there this afternoon, after school.

Gin Hmmm.

Dalton Name's Pace Creagan. We watched the train come through.

Gin Boy got killed up there a couple of years ago.

Dalton It's not a big train but it's big up close. And loud.

Gin You kiss her?

Dalton No way. She's not the kissing kind. Not pretty either.

Gin (*matter-of-factly*) Not that handsome yourself, Dalton.

Dalton That's what she said.

Gin I know the Creagans. They're all right.

Dalton Even if I wanted to, and I'm not saying I do, I never really – you know, like how people do – kissed a girl.

Gin Not much to it. Just open your mouth and start chewing. First time I kissed your father it was all wet and disgusting. By the second time I'd started to like him, and then it was like breathing water for air, that smooth.

Dalton I don't know.

Gin Neither did I.

> *Dray appears. He sits in a corner with a stool. No one speaks for some moments. Dray just sits with his back*

*to them. As they speak Dalton walks over and lights
Dray's candle, casually; he does this all the time for
his father.*

Dalton I need some new shoes.

Gin I know that.

Dalton I'll get a job.

Gin You've got school.

Dray makes a hand shadow on the wall.

And no one's hiring.

Dalton You know, the train that comes through Pope
Lick, the engine weighs one hundred and fifty-three tons.
That's what Pace says.

*Dray makes another. Dalton watches his father. He
moves to put his hand on his father's shoulder but his
father looks at him, like a warning, so Dalton
withdraws his hand.*

Gin Trains. Yeah. Huge, sweatin', steamin', oil-spittin'
promises when I was a girl. Always taking someone
away, never bringing someone back. I couldn't get used
to it.

Dalton I'm going out. (*He kisses his mother on the
cheek, then moves away.*) When you were fifteen. Like
me, Mother. What did you want?

Dray makes another hand shadow.

Gin Someone to look me straight in the face and tell me
flat out that I wasn't going anywhere.

Dalton Yeah? Well then, say it to me. Go on. Say it to
me.

Gin (*quietly*) Dalton.

Dalton Say: Dalton, my boy. You're not going anywhere.

Gin is silent, then:

Gin You're my child.

Dalton (*quietly*) That doesn't make any difference.

Dalton exits. Dray stops making hand shadows. He is still.

Gin (*just looks at Dray's back*) Touch me.

Dray is still. He turns to look at her, then slowly looks away.

SCENE FOUR

Pace and Dalton at the trestle, a few days later.

Pace We need to watch her for days and days. Studyin'. Studyin'. And then one night we'll run her.

Dalton Sure. One night.

Pace There's a simple reason we're biding our time. Waiting for the moment that counts: we don't want to die. Now repeat after me: 'We don't want to die.'

Dalton We don't want to die.

Pace So we'll be patient.

Dalton Yeah. Until Christmas. I'll be getting some new shoes. And then I'll hook a job. Move up.

Pace That's against the laws of gravity. Besides, you can't move up when you've got no teeth.

Dalton I've got teeth.

Pace You won't in a few years.

Dalton You've got no determination. No plan for the future.

Pace Yeah, but I watch.

Dalton Watch what?

Pace Things. People. I've been watching. Tomorrow. Today. For years. And this is how things are. You and me and the rest of us kids out here, we're just like. Okay. Like potatoes left in a box. You ever seen a potato that's been left in a box? The potato thinks the dark is the dirt and it starts to grow roots so it can survive, but the dark isn't the dirt and all it ends up sucking on is a fistful of air. And then it dies.

Dalton I'm not a potato.

Pace Yes you are.

Dalton No I'm not. Potatoes can't run. I can. And when we decide to do it, I'm gonna make it over that trestle before you're halfway across. Until then, I'm going home.

Pace What time is it?

Dalton Six fifty-one.

Pace Tell you what. We'll have a practice first.

Dalton What kind of practice?

Pace A real kind. Almost. Just to warm up. Pop the bones. Roll the blood over. You know.

Pace opens the paper bag she has with her. In it are a pair of boy's pants. She starts to take off her dress, not caring a bit that Dalton is there.

Dalton Jesus.

Pace Would you practise running the trestle in a dress?

Dalton turns around.

You can look if you want.

Dalton No thanks. You're not my type.

Pace continues changing.

Pace (*casually*) Why not?

Dalton You're loud. Your hands are dirty. You stare. (*Beat.*) And you're not pretty, really.

Pace You said that before.

Dalton Well, it keeps coming back to me.

Pace Anything else, kid?

Dalton There'll be more once I get to know you.

Pace I'm ready.

Dalton turns around. Pace is dressed in pants and a shirt, perhaps her brother's. She throws the dress at Dalton.

Smell it.

Dalton No way.

Pace Baby.

Dalton smells the dress.

Well?

Dalton It smells nice. Flowery. Like a girl.

Pace (*cuffs him as she snatches the dress back*) Want to know what I don't like about you, Dalton Chance? You're a good boy. A very good boy.

Dalton So what's that mean?

Pace It means someone, before it's too late, has got to break you in half. (*Sighs.*) I guess it'll have to be me.

SCENE FIVE

The present. Dalton in his cell, turned away from Chas.

Chas Now him over there, he doesn't know who's his mother. A turtle doesn't consider those things. Want to know how I know he's a turtle? (*Chas demonstrates, impressively, a turtle, moving his neck in and out of his shell.*) I know what you're thinking: could be a goose. I thought of that. But a goose doesn't do this – (*Chas moves his head slowly from side to side, then cocks his head to one side, opens his mouth and eats.*) A goose doesn't eat like a turtle. How you feelin', boy? What're you thinking? Still won't talk. Still won't talk. But they got it on record when they brought you in: 'Yeah, I killed her.' That's what you said. Why didn't you lie? They don't have a witness. Four words. Just four words: 'Yeah, I killed her.' But won't say why. Won't say how. What kind of a game are you playing? Well, they'll find it out. They know about kids. I had a boy your age. Couple of years older than you. Not much to him. But he was my son. (*Beat.*) To think. He was just a kid like you. Scared of nothing. Yeah. Scared of nothing 'cause you are nothing. Half of you kids wanting to kill, the rest wanting to die. Ordering death like it's a nice, cold drink and you're going to suck it down in one gulp and then get up and walk away from it. Right. Kids. Just want to eat, fuck and tear the ornaments off the tree. But only if you don't have to get out of bed in the morning to do it. The whole damn country's going to hell 'cause of your kind. (*Beat.*) You should have killed your own self instead. That's what they say. (*Beat.*) I loved my boy Brett. But I never could figure what he was. Something kinda small. Like a wheel, maybe. Something that spins in place in the dark. He had a gap in his heart. He was empty. I know; I was his father.

Sometimes he'd ask me to embrace him. (*Shrugs.*) He was my son. (*Beat.*) So he'd be here, in my arms, sniffling like a baby. But there was nothing. I was holding him. He was in my arms. But it was like holding onto. Nothing. (*Beat.*) What's it feel like to be like that? Huh? What's it feel like to be that empty? (*Begins to take off his shirt.*) I'm going to have to hate you, I guess. There's not much choice.

Chas stands over Dalton. Dalton is shivering and does not respond. Chas puts his shirt around Dalton.

I'll bring you some dinner. You've lost weight. Hard not to do in here.

SCENE SIX

Pace, Dalton and Gin are sitting together. There is a strained feeling. Dalton wants things to be okay, nice.

Gin Dalton made a clock for his science project. Didn't you, Dalton?

Dalton That was last year. This year I made a scale. To measure things on.

Gin A scale. That's right. I use it in the kitchen. To measure flour. It works really well. You want to try it, Pace?

Pace I don't do much with flour.

Gin Oh. (*Beat.*) But I'm sure you help your mother in the kitchen.

Dalton speaks before Pace can answer.

Dalton Pace likes to sew. Don't you?

Pace just looks at Dalton.

She makes her own clothes. Tell her you make your own clothes, Pace.

Pace I make my own clothes. My mother's not what she used to be.

Gin That's nice. I mean, about your clothes. What did your mother use to be?

Pace Hopeful. (*Beat.*) Thank you for the tea, Mrs Chance. It was very sweet.

Gin That's how we like it here. In our home.

They all sit in an awkward silence. After some moments, Pace places the large bag she's brought on the table.

Dalton Pace said she brought something for you, Mother.

Gin My, that's nice. You didn't need to, really.

Pace I made it in science class. Like Dalton did. (*Pace unwraps the bag to reveal a strange mechanical engine. It looks impressive.*)

Gin Oh. That's. Nice. What is it?

Pace It's a beam engine.

Gin I see . . .

Pace The beam engine was the first practical working steam engine. It's simple: fire here at the bottom heats the water, the steam forces up the piston and it's cooled, fast, by spraying cold water on the cylinder. This turns the steam back to water and makes a vacuum in the space under the piston.

Gin Piston.

Dalton It's a present, Mother.

Pace You see, the pressure of air outside the cylinder then pushes the piston back down again. And so on. The crosspiece joining the engine to the pump gives it its name: 'beam' engine.

Gin This is a train you've got here?

Pace An engine. But it's an older model.

Gin Looks kind of small to me.

Pace The original was bigger than both of us.

Gin Well, start it up then.

Pace Doesn't work. Did once. Second time, my father he was leaning over it to have a look, caught his beard on fire. Third time: bang. Not a big one, but I got a piece of glass in my arm.

Gin Sounds unpredictable.

Pace It's the only thing I had of my own to give you. (*Beat.*) I didn't get a good grade on it.

Gin You're two years older than Dalton.

Dalton Mother.

Pace Almost.

Gin He's been seeing a lot of you these past weeks.

Dalton Can we have some more tea?

Pace You ever hear of Cugnot, Mrs Chance? Nicholas Cugnot. Made the first steam machine that moved. Crawled two m.p.h. before it blew up. That was in France. Seventeen sixty-nine, I think. The government put Cugnot in prison. Explosion didn't hurt anyone. Never understood why they put him in jail.

Gin My son doesn't know a thing about trains.

Pace I think they were afraid. Not of the machine, but of Cugnot. They'd never seen anything like that moved by steam. Just plain old water – (*Makes the sound of steam.*) – into steam. It must have shaken them up somehow. Just to see it. They couldn't forgive him.

Gin What do you want with Dalton?

Dalton Christ. We're just having tea.

Gin Hush up.

Dalton shuts up. He puts his head in his hands.

We're a family here, Pace. A regular family. My husband, Dalton and me. Lots of trouble out there, lots of bad weather. But we take care of each other; nothing out there we need. I want you to know that.

Pace You know the Union Pacific? They're gonna build the biggest steam locomotives in the world. The engine and tender'll weigh over five hundred tons. Colossal. They'll be 4–8–8–4 articulated locomotives with two sets of driving wheels, each with their own cylinders.

Gin just stares at her.

I'm sorry, Mrs Chance. But me and Dalton. It's none of your business.

Gin Cylinders, huh? Driving wheels. Articulated locomotives. If you're thinking to trick my son –

Dalton I can't believe this . . .

Pace Mrs Chance, I'm not sweet on your son's locomotive system, if that's what you mean. We've never touched each other. I've got nothing to be ashamed of. Though I did tell him to take off his clothes once, under the trestle.

Gin To take off his –

Dalton Pace!

Pace (*interrupts*) Shut up, Dalton. (*Beat.*) And then once on the tracks. A hundred feet up. Wasn't a train in sight. It was kinda chilly that evening, but it was safe.

Gin I think you better leave now.

Pace He doesn't like me, really. He says I'm loud.

Gin (*to Dalton*) You took off your clothes?

Pace He's your son. He does what he's told.

Gin Why would you do such a thing? Anyone might have seen you.

Pace Yeah. I did. And he's not like an engine at all. Nah. Dalton's pale. Real pale. No steam. How's he keep warm? Doesn't know the first thing about cylinders. And he's so light, what keeps him where he stands? On the tracks, slip, slip, slip. No traction. Now, the Big Boys, the new ones, they'll need near ten tons of coal per hour in their firebox. And the grate where the coal'll be burned is bigger than a kitchen.

Ginny just stares at her.

Imagine it. That's what we're coming to.

SCENE SEVEN

Dalton and Pace at the trestle.

Pace Let's start here. On this tie.

Dalton What tie? The track's up there.

Pace Imagine it, stupid.

Dalton Right.

Pace See, this tie's marked with a red X.

Dalton Maybe I want to start on this other tie.

Pace Look. It's tradition, okay. Besides, Brett made this X, so let's use it. Now, you crouch down like this. Go on. Yeah. That's right. Like at a track meet. Point your skinny rear to the stars. Got it.

Dalton I'll count down.

Pace Now when you say, 'Go,' we run like crazy to the other side. But don't check your feet. You'll trip if you check your feet. Just trust that your feet know where to go.

Dalton I hear you.

Pace You're playin' chicken with the train so you keep your eyes on the engine headed towards you. It'll look like she's real close but she won't be. If you start when I tell you to, you'll have enough time to make it across and have dinner before she starts over the trestle. Ready?

Dalton Pace?

Pace Yeah?

Dalton My legs are shaking.

Pace This is practice, Dalton. There's no train down here.

Dalton My legs aren't so sure.

Pace On the count of three. Come on.

Dalton and Pace One, two, three –

Dalton Wait! (*Dalton seems to be looking over an edge.*)

Pace Don't look. You'll lose your nerve.

Dalton It's a long way down.

Pace Why don't we just walk it? Give me your hand. (*Pace takes his hand and begins to walk him.*)

Dalton God we're high up.

Pace (*smacks him*) Keep your eyes on the other side. Pretend that we're running.

They pretend they're running, and run in place.

Dalton We are. I'm out of breath.

Pace We're almost there. Yeah. Yeah. Grease those knees. And now you trip.

Dalton What?

Pace You trip.

Pace trips him so he falls to the ground.

Dalton Hey! What the – You tripped me. Hey –

Pace It might happen.

Dalton Why'd you –

Dalton tries to get up. She knocks him back down, hard.

Pace You might trip. Anything's possible. We got to be ready for it.

Dalton But I wouldn't've tripped! You pushed me!

Pace Don't get up. Just sit there. Like you tripped. Let's say I'm flaggin' behind and you look over your shoulder to see how I'm doing and you trip. And just as you trip you hear her coming around the hill. (*Pace makes the sound of a train whistle.*)

Dalton You sound like a kitten. It's like this. (*Dalton makes an even better and more frightening whistle.*)

Pace Yeah! And you can hear her cold slathering black hell of a heart barrelling towards the trestle and it sounds like this –

Together they make an engine sound, surprisingly well.

Pace But you've twisted your ankle.

Dalton Yeah. And I can hardly stand. It feels like my foot's coming off. (*Makes a painful gasp.*) I try to run but I can only hobble. And the train, she's just about to cross.

Pace And then there I am. At your side.

Dalton No. I'd slow you down and you know it. You just pass me by. (*Makes the sound of an arrow flying.*) Like an arrow. You've got to save your own skin.

Pace Yeah, but I can't just leave you there.

Dalton Yes you can.

Pace You'll be killed.

Dalton I'll be torn apart.

Pace So I put my arm around your waist and start to drag you down the tracks with me. It's hard going. We've only got fifty feet or so 'til we're clear.

Dalton But the train. (*Dalton lets out the terrible scream of a whistle.*) So you drop me.

Pace No.

Dalton You drop me and run. You run for your life.

Pace No. I don't leave you. I –

Dalton You make it across. Just in time. Alone.

Pace I drag you with me.

Dalton And as you clear the tracks, you feel the hurtling wind of her as she rushes by you, so close it's like she's kissing the back of your neck, so close she pulls the shirt right up off you without popping the buttons. (*Beat.*) And then? And then you hear me scream.

Dalton lets out a terrible scream and at the same time Pace screams:

Pace I save you!

They are silent for some moments.

Dalton And then? And then nothing. The train, she disappears over the trestle and on down the track. (*Beat.*) You, Pace Creagan, are standing there, breathing hard –

Pace – my heart jumping jacks, yeah, shooting dice in my chest. Snake eyes. But I'm alive. Alive!

Dalton As for me, well, you know I'm dead. You're certain. But still you have to go back and have a look. To see what's left. Of course there's almost nothing left.

Pace Yeah there was. There was a lot left.

Dalton No. Just some bits of. Meat. And a running shoe. That's all. I'm mashed potatoes now. Just add some milk and stir.

Pace He wasn't wearing running shoes.

Dalton Hey. Take a look at my face. I'm talking to you: I'm dead.

Pace Brett was wearing boots.

Dalton And now maybe my mom will be able to scrounge up some new shoes for the funeral. If she can find my feet.

Pace (*calmly*) Shut up. Just. Shut up. Have you ever put a shell up to your ear?

Dalton What?

Pace A conch shell. One of those big ones. It's not the ocean you're hearing. Or even the blood in your head.

(*Makes the sound of a shell over one's ear.*) That's the sound. You know it. And it's been going on for years. Even now you can hear it. Listen. It's this town. Our future. You and me. (*Makes the sound again.*) Empty. No more, no less. Just. Empty.

Dalton (*disgusted*) I'm going home.

Pace Wait.

Dalton (*leaving*) Not this time.

Pace Take off your clothes.

Dalton Why?

Pace Because you want to.

> *Dalton begins to undress. Pace watches him. He's about to take off his underwear.*

Stop. There. Yeah. That's enough.

> *They both watch each other. Pace moves closer to him, but not that close.*

Are you cold?

Dalton A little. (*Beat.*) Well. Are you gonna touch me or what?

Pace No. I just wanted. To look at you.

Dalton Once you take your clothes off. Something is supposed to happen.

Pace It already has. (*Beat.*) Get dressed.

> *After a moment, Dalton starts to get dressed.*

SCENE EIGHT

Gin and Dray. He sits immobile. She uncovers a small stack of plates. She tosses one to him. Suddenly he comes alive and they are tossing a plate back and forth between them as they speak. They've done this before.

Gin You've got to get out.

Dray I'm movin'. You just can't see it.

Gin At the WPA office. They're helpin' people find jobs.

Dray A handful.

Gin That's better than nothing.

Dray I don't know.

Gin I went by the council. They got kicked out of the church basement. Got a room in the Watson storehouse. More like a closet than a room.

Dray The council. They're not government.

Gin No, they're not. Just people out of work. Tryin' to get things going. Lots of talk about the plate glass factory.

Dray It's closed down.

Gin Talk about opening it up again. Building it back up. Running it themselves. Machinery's still there. Most of it. It's a mess, but it's all still there.

Dray We've got what we need. The three of us. Under this roof.

Gin I know that.

Dray Sounds like you're getting involved.

Gin No. I'm not. I'm just listening.

Dray My father worked there when he was a boy. There'd be explosions now and then. He wore eye wear. A lot of them didn't. Once the glass hit him in the mouth. Long thin pieces of glass. He pulled them out his cheeks with pliers, like pullin' fish bones out a fish. (*Beat.*) That place doesn't belong to them, Gin. Sounds like communists.

Gin People, Dray. Just people tired of not working. Tired of waiting for the WPA to hand out the jobs. Tired. Just tired. You know that kind of tired.

Dray Can't remember when I wasn't.

Gin I remember. When you were a boy.

Dray almost drops a plate, but catches it. He becomes more playful.

Dray You lie, Miss Ginny Carol. I was never a kid.

Gin Yeah you were. And so was I.

Dray Nah. That was just a fancy idea we had about ourselves.

Gin You didn't bring me flowers like other girls got. You brought me tomatoes.

Dray You can't eat flowers.

Gin And corn. You were nineteen.

Dray A bucket of frogs, too. I made you close your eyes and put your hands in it. You didn't scream like most of them did. You went dead pale. I thought I might have killed you. And then you did the damnedest thing: you kissed me. Not on the cheek, either. Smack on the mouth.

Gin I was in shock. The frogs did it to me. (*Beat.*) You hardly kissed me back.

Dray I was in shock. Never had a girl put her tongue in my mouth before. We weren't even engaged. You took me to the storm shelter and took off your dress. You pushed me to my knees. I never kissed a girl there before. I never even thought it could be done. You went dead pale. That was the second time I thought I killed you. When you finally let me get to my feet, you had a clump of my hair in each of your hands, you'd pulled on my head so hard.

Gin I wasn't tired back then. And neither were you.

Dray No, I guess I wasn't. (*Beat.*) There were two things I wanted when I was a boy: one was to land a good job at the foundry, the other was to have you turn me into a bald man by the time I was old.

Gin You lost quite a bit of hair over the years. Though not lately, I'm sorry to say.

Dray misses a plate, which drops and breaks. Silence.

Dray It was mine, Gin. Nineteen years of it.

Gin Yeah, and what did it give you? A bad arm, a broken collar, burns across your back so deep the bath water stays in them.

Dray That job was mine.

Gin We're still here.

Dray Yeah. And you won't ever leave me.

Gin I won't ever leave you, Dray.

Silence for some moments.

I heard at work they were hiring a couple of men down at Turner's. You might –

Dray (*interrupts*) I was there this morning while you were at work. They hired three men. Three men. Fifty-two of us they left standing. There wasn't a sound. For the longest time we just stood there watching the door that'd been shut. All that disappointment. Fifty-two men. Fifty-two of us. And weighin' how much? None of us eating big these days. Most of us lookin' lean. Maybe . . . nine thousand pounds, all of us together. That much disappointment. (*Beat.*) And not a sound.

> *Dray sits with the plate in his lap. They sit in silence some moments. Gin moves to touch Dray, to comfort him. Dray speaks gently to her.*

Don't touch me, Gin. I could kill you.

SCENE NINE

Dalton lying asleep on the floor in a blanket. He gets up. He is shirtless. He thinks he's alone. But Gin is standing over him; he starts.

Gin Dalton.

Dalton You're always alone.

Gin He hardly leaves the house.

Dalton You'd think this might be special circumstances.

Gin He's restless. Without you home.

Dalton He never looked me over when I was there.

Gin You don't have to look at someone –

Dalton I don't need your excuses. Neither does he. From what I remember, he didn't look at you any more than he did at me.

Gin Not long ago he used to hold me.

Dalton Big deal. Holding someone's a cinch. You just open your arms, pop them inside, then open again and you're done. It doesn't cost. It's easy.

Gin And the girl. What about her, then? To hold her?

Pace appears. While neither Gin nor Dalton sees her, sometimes they sense, at different moments, that she is 'there'. Pace is playful.

Was that 'easy'?

Dalton That's none of your business. (*Beat.*) I don't want you here.

Pace Was that 'a cinch'?

Dalton (*shouts*) I didn't hold her! (*Now he is quiet.*) She held me. Pace did. But it wasn't that. Holding. Sometimes when I was with her, she wasn't there. Or when I was without her, she was there, but not there. Alone at night in bed, I could feel her breath in my ears. No.

Pace and Dalton That's not it.

Pace It wasn't just you and me.

Dalton It was something more. Like at school. At school they teach you. To speak. They say it's math –

Pace – history –

Dalton – geometry, whatever. But they're teaching you to speak. Not about the world but about things. Just things: a door, a map –

Pace – a cup. Just the name of it.

Dalton Not what a cup means, who picked it up, who drank from it –

Pace – who didn't and why –

Dalton – where a map came from, who fixed in the rivers, who'll take the wrong turn; or a door. Who cut the wood and hung it there? Why that width, that height? And who made that decision? Who agreed to it? Who didn't?

Pace And what happened to them because of it?

Dalton They just teach us to speak the things. So that's what we speak. But there's no past that way.

Pace and Dalton And no future.

Dalton 'Cause after you've said the thing, you move on. You don't look back. You never think to cross it, never stop and turn.

Pace (*no longer playful*) But you stopped, didn't you, Dalton? You stopped and turned.

Dalton She laughed at everything that seemed right.

Pace And you didn't turn back. (*calmly*) You son of a bitch. (*Pace retreats somewhat, but she is still 'there'.*)

Dalton It wasn't just at night. In the day sometimes. Not her voice but the sound of her. I could hear it. Like water running in a pipe. Coal shifting in the grate. But that's not it. It was more like this. This cup. (*Dalton takes his drinking cup, calmly kneels and breaks it on the floor. His hand bleeds slightly. He sorts through the pieces.*) Look. This was sand and heat. Not long ago. Other things, too. Pieces and bits. And now. It's something else. Glass. Blood. And it's broken. (*He picks up a large piece, nears Gin.*) I could cut you open with it.

   Gin slaps him in the face. He's taken aback, put in his place.

Dalton But that's what she did to me. Cut me open and things weren't just things after that. They were more. What they'd once been and what they could be besides. I was just a kid –

Pace – like any other. You didn't care.

Dalton I never even thought about it. But then one day I wasn't sure. She did that to me. She made me – hesitate.

In everything I did. I was. Unsure. Look. It's not a cup any more; it's a knife.

Pace stands close to Dalton, but he cannot see her.

Pace I could cut you open and see my face.

Dalton And it was true. I could touch myself at night and I didn't know if it was her hand or mine. I could touch myself. I could put my hand. I could. Maybe I was asleep. I don't know but sometimes I put my hand. Inside myself.

Pace (*whispers to him*) And you were wet.

Dalton I was wet. Just like a girl. It was. Yeah. Like I was touching her. Just to touch myself. (*Beat.*) It wasn't right.

Silence for some moments.

Gin Only time I ever knew things were right is when they were wrong. Everyone said your father was a mistake. After I made that one, and it worked out so well, I dedicated myself to making as many mistakes as possible in a lifetime. The only time I was ever sure who I was was when I was wrong. (*Beat.*) I think you loved that girl.

Dalton Yeah. Maybe that's why I killed her. Please. I want you to go.

Gin All right.

Pace suddenly kicks a piece of the broken cup. It skids between Gin and Dalton. Gin looks at the broken piece. Split scene: Dray is alone in another area. Perhaps up above them. In the dark. He is making awkward but somehow lovely movements about the room. Then we see he is dancing without music.

Pace There's your cup, kid. Drink from it.

Then Dray sings and dances his song:

Dray
When I was still living, when I was a boy
I could sing like the water and dance like a toy.
My love she would kiss me 'til my mouth it was warmed.
There was no place on earth where we'd ever be harmed.

SCENE TEN

Pace and Dalton under the trestle.

Dalton There's no one home at my house in the daytime.
We could hang out there. Well, my dad's at home but
I'm not sure he counts as someone any more. Ever since
he got laid off at the foundry, he sits with the lights off.
He's got a candle burning. Makes shadows on the wall
with his hands. Spiders. Bats. You know. Rabbits.

Pace I guess I'm supposed to think that's sad.

Dalton You think about kissing me?

Pace Kissing you where?

Dalton I don't know. Here. In your yard. Or mine.

Pace I mean where on you?

Dalton My mouth. Where else?

Pace Nope. We're friends.

Dalton Like you and Brett were friends?

Pace That was different. He was like my sister or
something.

Dalton Yeah. Yeah. Just forget it, okay. Pace Creagan
isn't that kind of girl, anyhow. She pulls knives. She
takes off her clothes. She pisses under the trestle.

Pace Shits there too. I mean, why go all the way home?

Dalton But she doesn't think about kissing.

Pace Not on the mouth; that's common.

Dalton Where else then?

Pace I don't know. A place where no one else has kissed you, maybe. Everyone in the world has kissed you on the face, right?

Dalton Keep talking.

Pace If I ever kiss you, and I'm not saying I ever will, it will be some place even you've never thought of.

Dalton You mean – (*Dalton looks down at his crotch, with a sort of nervous bravado.*)

Pace No way. You could trick me and piss on me. Look, if you want a kiss so bad, I'll give it to you, but you got to promise to take it wherever I want to plant it.

Dalton If it's at least ten seconds long, I promise.

Pace Agreed. Take down your pants.

Dalton (*suddenly afraid*) No. Wait. You said it wasn't there!

Pace It's not. Trust me.

   With some apprehension, Dalton drops his pants.

Turn around.

Dalton Pace. I'm not sure –

Pace (*interrupts*) Shut up, kid. We got a deal.

   Dalton reluctantly turns around. Pace stands behind him, then drops to her knees.

Count.

45

Pace puts her mouth just above the back of his knee. She kisses him there and holds it.

Dalton One, two, three, four, five, six . . . seven . . .

Pace slaps him and he continues counting.

. . . eight, nine, ten.

Pace stands up. Dalton pulls up his pants. They look at each other.

Dalton Well. Yeah.

Pace You happy now?

Dalton Happy. Sure. (*Beat.*) I'm gonna run over to my friend Sean's right now and tell him all about it. How it was great. How long it lasted. How far we went. 'Sean, Sean, guess what? She tongued the back of my knee!' Is that what you did with your friend Brett? You kiss him like that too?

Pace approaches him, then spits on him and wipes her mouth.

Pace There. You can have it back. I wish I'd never done it.

Dalton starts to push her. He's pushing her hard backwards but she keeps her footing. The potential for violence to escalate is evident.

Dalton Spit on me? You think you can do that? Who the hell do you think you are? Who the hell, Pace Creagan? What's so special about your kiss, huh? I could just take it, you know. I could just take it if I wanted to.

Now Pace pushes back. Dalton hesitates. Pace raises her arm to hit him but then hesitates.

Dalton Go on. I'm your friend. Hit me.

Pace I don't want to hit you. I want you to shut up. You liked it. I could tell. You're mad at me 'cause you liked it.

46

Dalton I wanted you to kiss me on the mouth.

Pace When you were counting. All the while. Couldn't you feel it? Where I was kissing you, it was on your mouth.

They are quiet for some moments.

Dalton What I said about Brett. It was stupid.

Pace Yeah. It was. (*Beat.*) But you were wrong the other day. That's not what a train does to you. It doesn't mush you up in neat little pieces. This train. She's a knife. That's why we loved her. Me and Brett. This train, you've seen her. So much beauty she's breathless: a huge hunk and chunk of shiny black coal blasted fresh out of the mountain. (*Beat.*) We had a good start. Me and Brett. We both could have made it. 'Course Brett, he was faster. I expected to be running behind. But Brett was worried. About me. He was stupid like that. He turned to look over his shoulder at me and he tripped. I thought he'd just jump up and keep going so I passed him right by. We'd timed it tight, and right then that engine was so close I could smell her. (*Beat.*) I thought Brett was right behind me.

Dalton You left him on the tracks?

Pace I thought he was running behind me. I could hear him behind me. He didn't call out. He didn't say wait up. I didn't know. Why didn't he call out?

There is the real sound of a whistle in the distance.

Not even a sound. Brett just sat there where he'd fallen. And then he stood up, slowly, like he had the time. He stood there looking at her, looking her straight in the face. Almost like it was a dare. Like: 'Go ahead and hit me.' You can't do that to a train. You can't dare a train to hit you. 'Cause it will.

47

Another whistle, closer this time.

Dalton This is stupid. Brett was alone up there. Nobody knows.

Pace Just stood there like she could pass right through him for all he cared. Like he wasn't going to flinch.

Dalton Let's get out of here, it's getting late. (*He takes her arm.*)

Pace Let go of me.

Dalton You're making this up.

Pace Get off.

Dalton You're out of your mind.

Dalton tries to grab her again. She resists and he stumbles. There is the sound of a train rushing over the trestle above them. The sound is huge. Then it disappears into the distance. He's cut his hand.

Shit.

Pace You all right?

Dalton No. Cut my hand.

Pace Let me see.

Dalton Just a scratch.

Pace It's not how you think it is. The train, she doesn't mush you up. An arm here. A leg here. A shoe. No. She's cleaner than that. I walked back down the tracks after the train had passed. She cut Brett in two.

Dalton Pace.

Pace You know what I thought? Blocks. Two blocks, and maybe if I could fit the pieces back together again, he'd be. Whole.

48

Dalton Will you shut your mouth. Please.

Pace (*ripping a strip of cloth from her dress to bandage his hand*) Use this. Wrap it around your hand. It'll stop the bleeding.

Dalton Thanks. (*Beat.*) You going home now?

Pace I don't know. My mom made a loaf for my brother's birthday tomorrow. Maybe we could weasel some out of her tonight.

Dalton Okay.

Pace We're going to do it for real.

Dalton Yeah. We'll do it. We'll make the cross.

Pace Both of us. Side by side.

Dalton That's right.

Pace A steady run.

Dalton As can be.

Pace Does your dad really make shadow animals on the wall?

Dalton Yep.

Pace Can you?

Dalton Never tried.

Pace That's pretty neat. Not everyone can do that. I can't.

Pace stands close to him, face to face for a moment.

You won't take anything from me that I don't want to give you, Dalton. And that's a fact.

Dalton All right. (*Beat.*) Hey, I'll race you down the hill.

Pace Nah. I'm tired. (*Beat.*) Go!

Blackout. We hear Dalton's voice in the dark, but as though it were coming from a distance away.

Dalton Hey, you – I'll catch you this time!

SCENE ELEVEN

In the semi-dark we see only the hands of someone. Two, blue hands. They move about in the dark. They 'play'. As though someone were hesitantly trying out their glow in the dark. Suddenly, Pace appears, perhaps somewhere above or behind Gin. Pace is in the same dress as in her earlier encounters with Dalton. The tear in the dress is larger. This is the only difference in her appearance. Though Pace is not in front of Gin, Gin speaks to her and looks at her as though Pace were right in front of her.

Gin Oh. Pace.

Pace is still. She just watches Gin.

I didn't see you. I was just. Trying to get used to this. It won't come off. They're lights, almost. It doesn't hurt. Well, it hurts 'cause I scrub them but it does no good. This colour's here to stay. One morning I go to work and I come home with blue hands. They changed chemicals again at the plant. All sixteen of us in my section got blue hands. Some of the women, they were upset when it wouldn't wash off. But we had to see it as a wonder, too. During break, we turned off the lights and standing all together, some with our arms raised, others at our side, we looked like a Christmas tree in the dark, with blue lights. Then we all put our arms over our heads like this (*demonstrates*) and waved our fingers and we were a flock of crazy blue birds taking off. We started laughing then, and piling on top of each other, imagine it, and most of us women my age, and our hands were like blue snowballs flying this way and that. One of the girls, Victoria, she laughed so hard she peed right where she stood. Another one, Willa, she slipped in it and that had all of us roaring. (*Beat.*) Then Laura Townsend said we had all better think again 'cause we had the hands of dead women. Well, that put an end to the fun and we went back to work. The manager said it would wear off but it won't. We even used bleach. We'll have to get used to it. Kind of ugly and kind of pretty both, isn't it? But hands aren't meant to be blue. (*Beat.*) You're almost a woman yourself, Pace. Hell, I don't blame him. My husband. We're not. Close. Do you know what I mean? Like we used to be.

Pace You asked me what I wanted with your son.

Gin I meant no harm, girl. A mother's supposed to ask.

Pace I was going to be different. I don't know in what way. That never mattered. But different somehow. Do you know what I mean?

Gin There's blood on your leg.

Pace And Dalton would be there to see it happen. That's what I was getting him ready for.

Gin What are you doing out so late? Where's Dalton?

Pace He'll be home. He's still out at the trestle. (*Beat.*) He's not alone. He's with a girl.

Gin Oh. Pace. I'm sorry.

Pace I'm not. I was watching them. At first, I couldn't see them. It was dark. And there was this noise, like water rushing. Right through my head. But then I looked harder and I could see them. He stood over her. He was shaking her. But she wouldn't get up. And he was shouting. Shouting so loud. He wouldn't shut up.

Gin Dalton wouldn't – No. Dalton's –

Pace (*interrupts*) But she wouldn't answer him. The girl just turned her head. She hates him, I thought. And that made me glad. And then he stopped shouting. He gave up and put his head on her breast. (*Beat.*) And then, well. I saw it; he kissed her. He kissed her.

Gin There'll be other boys, Pace –

Pace And she let him. I never let Dalton kiss me, but she did. And then, I felt him kiss her. I felt it. He was kissing her. Kissing her. But his mouth was inside of mine. And I let him. I let his mouth be inside of me like that, even though I wasn't with him any more.

Gin (*moving to comfort Pace*) Come here, girl. I'm sorry.

Pace (*stepping backwards*) Don't touch the back of my head.

Gin Why not?

Pace It's gone.

> We hear a door slam loudly.

Gin Dalton? Dalton!

> We hear the loud slamming of the door, like a cell. The slamming echoes.

> End of Act One.

Act Two

SCENE ONE

It's dark in Dalton's cell but then a light appears. It's Chas. Dalton lies sleeping on the ground. Chas stands over Dalton, watching Dalton sleep.

Chas Least you could do is turn into a boat. A little one. No oars. I could guess it. I know water.

> *Dalton moans in his sleep, like a child. Chas sings to put Dalton back to sleep.*

> Rocking on the sea, looking for my soul
> Dead man's blood from an old boat hole.
> Sail to the left, sail to the right,
> Sail to the end in the cold moon light.

Sleep of the dead. That's you. Creagan. Pace. Ring a bell? In the dead. Of night. What're you thinkin'? Are you there with her or somewhere else? (*Standing over Dalton, Chas begins to peel an apple. Chas lets the bits of peel fall across Dalton's face.*) Why do I spend my time on you, huh? Could it be I know our friend across the hall is on his way out of here? The poor man's got no wind in his jail cell. Still, he's doing this – (*Chas spins his head to the left and right like a weathervane.*) He's a weathervane tonight. (*Beat.*) I'm waiting for you to surprise me, kid. Turn your head, open your mouth, roll your eyes, swish your feet and I'll know it: you're a fish of sorts. Could you do that? Here? Or am I wastin' time, my time, when I could be over the sea fightin' with the Abe Lincoln, bullets and dive-bombers whistlin' and divin' and you here, sweet as baby's breath, sleeping and moaning over a dead girl. And I'm sharing my apple.

What are county jails coming to? (*Softly chants.*)

Apples, apples, buy a veteran's apples,
Sweet and hard as ruby rocks.
Five cents apiece, two dollars for a box.
Apples, apples, buy an old man's apples.
Fought for his country, left on his back.
Won't you taste his apples, they're black, black, black?

Whatever you are, my boy, I'll find you out. I won't sleep.
And little by little, you'll stop sleeping, too.

*The peel falling on his face finally wakes Dalton and
he screams himself awake. He sits up, not knowing
where he is.*

Another one, kid. That's about three a night now. You're
sweating 'til you stink. Hey. I got a good one. What's
this? (*Chas gets down on all fours and acts out something
contorted and disturbing.*) Come on. Make a wild guess.
I'll give you a buck. And a hint: it's something you can't
see, but it's there from the moment you're born 'til the
moment you die. What is it?

*Chas repeats the act. This time it's more grotesque. He
comes up close to Dalton, too close and Dalton backs
away, frightened.*

Give up? (*Beat.*) It's your soul.

After some moments:

Dalton Go to hell.

Chas He speaks! He speaks! And what does he tell me?
Go to hell. Go to hell. That's us in here, isn't it? Just you
and me, hour after hour. So tell me. Tell me. Why'd you
kill her? Think she was pregnant? Well, she wasn't. But
they say you got a chance if you say you thought she
was. Don't you want a chance, Chance? (*Beat.*) Why'd
you kill Pace Creagan?

54

Dalton Don't. Say her name.

Chas Pretty name. Strange. Strange girl, too. Lucky she wasn't more of a girl. More of a girl, and they'd hang you for sure. That's what they're saying. Seen her parents since? No. But I have. Like two grey sticks, the man and the wife, so thin with grief they are. As they walk, the wind blows them from one side of the road to the other. You did that to them. You did that, boy. She was a kid. A box of crackers. You opened her up, took a handful and threw the rest away.

Dalton gets to his feet.

That's it, boy. That's it. Let's see some life in you. I know what's inside of you. I know what's inside. Don't think I don't know. Here? (*Chas throws the small knife down on the floor between them.*) There it is, boy. You can use it. Go on. Show me what you really are. What happened that night, huh? Lose your nerve? You tried though. We know that. Dress all torn up. Head smashed. She must have put up a hell of a fight. I bet you liked that. That's the way you kids like it. All that fightin' hoists your flag, gets you flappin'. Got you so edged, you couldn't hold it in. Couldn't wait. Shot your cum all over her dress but missed the target. Oh yeah. It was your cum all right. But Pace Creagan died a virgin. That's what the doctor says.

Dalton moves away from Chas. After some moments, Chas picks up the knife. He speaks gently.

You want to kill me, don't you?

Dalton shakes his head, 'no'.

Chas I can see the hate rising out the top of your head like steam. Here, take this. Go on. (*He holds out the knife.*) You got to face up to what you are. You're a killer. A kid with a shell for a heart. A head full of black water. Everything sunk. Everything drowned inside you.

Chas forces Dalton to hold the knife. Chas forces the knife up to his own throat. Dalton is passive. Chas whispers.

Go on. It's what makes you whole.

Chas laughs softly. Then suddenly Dalton shouts and forces Chas backwards. Dalton forces Chas to the floor with the knife to his neck.

Dalton I don't want to do it. You're just a man. (*It seems as though Dalton could kill Chas any moment.*) I can't even imagine it. Killing someone like you. With her. With Pace. I could imagine it. This what you want to hear? Okay, then. Like her parents, she was just a stick. I picked her up, carried her a little ways, and when I got tired I broke her – snap – in half. Threw the pieces to the side. Those are the facts. It was that easy. You want a reason? Okay: the only way to love someone is to kill them.

Dalton releases Chas. But as he moves away, Chas suddenly grabs at his leg. Dalton attempts to shake him off, even drag him, but Chas holds on, lying on his belly. This makes for an irritating – and to us, comical – interruption for Dalton's words.

God damn it I did what I was told – (*Drags Chas a little way.*) – became what I was taught: a man with a little piece of future, 'bout as big as a dime. Only there wasn't one – Let go of my leg – There never was for most of us. That was the plan and it never was ours. But I bought that plan anyway – Get off of me – 'Cause it was the only thing to buy. Those are the facts. This isn't about who we are. This isn't about what we wanted.

With effort, Dalton breaks free. Chas lies still on the floor, looking up at him.

My country loves me. That's why it's killing me. It's killing my father. Those are the facts. Those are the facts of love.

After some moments, Chas gets to his feet.

Chas You. You're not our children. We don't want you.

Dalton What you were making earlier? That wasn't my soul. (*Beat.*) That was yours.

SCENE TWO

Gin stands with her mother's blue plates behind her back. Dray has cornered her.

Dray Give them to me.

Gin Get out of this house and get your own. These were my mother's. I won't do it any more. The Salvation was out. The woman there says to me, 'What're you doing with all those plates, ma'am?' I said, 'There's no food any more. We eat them.' I went down the road. I stopped at the dump. Next thing I'm on my hands and knees, digging through garbage to find something for you to break. That's when I started laughing. Laughed so hard two rats flew out from under me.

Dray Just give me one.

Gin Not one. Not two. Not ever again.

Dray Gin.

Gin Go to the jail and visit your son. Get outside. Tear the bricks from the sidewalk if you have to. I don't care.

Dray I can't. I'm afraid.

Gin Of what?

Dray That if I go out, they won't be able to see me.

Gin Who? Who won't be able to see you?

Dray People. Out walking in the road.

Gin Yes they will.

Dray They'll walk right through me. (*Dray slowly takes off his shirt, seemingly unconsciously, while he speaks.*) My mother used to tell me, 'Dray. You are what you do.' In the foundry, it's no rest and you've always got a burn somewhere. I never minded. I was doing. I was part of the work. Part of the day. I was. I don't know. Burning. Freezing up. Inside that buzz. Melting down alongside thirty other men. But we were there. You could see us, and we weren't just making steel, we were. I don't know. We were. Making ourselves. We were. I was. All that. Movement. Movement. And now I do. Nothing. So. Then I am. What? Yeah. Nothing.

Gin Go talk to them. They understand. They'll listen.

Dray I won't have anything to do with that council. I know what they're up to. They're gonna take something that's not theirs. They're gonna break the law.

Gin Yeah, well sometimes you break the law or it breaks you.

Dray Red thoughts, Ginny.

Gin Yeah. My thoughts are red and my hands are blue.

Dray begins methodically to rip his shirt into pieces as he speaks. This is a violent act, but somehow he does it calmly, simply.

Dray They were running. Like all of us are. A few months back, up north. You know the story. (*Rips the* *cloth*.) A strike. Out on the street. Thousands of them. Doing something about it – (*Rips the cloth*.) Like you say. Republic Steel brought the police out. Ten men were killed. All of them strikers. (*Rips the cloth*.) Papers said the strikers started it. Weeks later. It got around. They were running away. (*Rips the cloth*.) The bullets hit them in the back.

Gin I never said I wasn't afraid.

Dray (*he's finished with his shirt, and is very calm*) You can go ahead now. If you want.

Gin Where?

Dray I don't know.

> *Gin carefully, hesitantly touches his bare arm. Dray closes his eyes. She touches his chest.*

You're cold, Gin.

> *She keeps touching him. Now his back.*

But it's nice. It almost burns. (*Beat*.) There. That's enough.

Gin I don't want to stop.

Dray I don't want to either.

Gin I want you to kiss me.

Dray I can't. I might hurt you.

Gin I don't care.

Dray (*gently*) Get away from me. (*He's suddenly furious*.) I want you. Can't you understand that? I want you and it's choking me. Look at me: I don't know how to belong to my life. To be here. Not knowing where here is any more. Am I here, Ginny? What you're looking at – is it me?

After some moments:

Gin I'm going into that plant with the rest of them. I'm going to work with glass. We're going to make it ours. But I'm a coward. If they come after us, I'll run too. But I won't live. Like this any more.

Dray You want me to leave?

Gin I want you to do something.

Dray I can't.

Gin (*calmly*) I love you. So. I'll leave you behind.

SCENE THREE

Pace and Dalton. Pace is dressed in her brother's clothes. Dalton holds out her dress to her. Something unsettling has happened between them, though we don't know what. Pace takes the dress, looks at it.

Dalton Pace. What was that? What just happened?

Pace You tell me.

Dalton That wasn't. No. That wasn't. Right.

Pace (*examining the dress*) You made it wet.

Dalton I'm sorry. I didn't mean to.

   Pace throws the dress aside.

Pace Dalton Chance, when we're grown up, I want to stand here with you and not be afraid. I want to know it will be okay. Tonight. Tomorrow. That when it's time to work, I'll have work. That when I'm tired, I can rest. Just those things. Shouldn't they belong to us?

Dalton What do you want from me?

Pace I want you to watch me, to tell me I'm here.

Dalton You're here. You don't need me to tell you.

Pace Yes I do. So watch me. Whatever I do. Take a good look. Make some notes. 'Cause one day I might come back here to find out who I was – and then you're going to tell me.

Dalton I don't. Damn it. I don't know what you mean.

Pace Look, it's simple –

Dalton (*interrupts*) Stop it. Every time we meet, afterwards, it's like pieces of me. Keep falling off. It shouldn't be that way, Pace. Something's got to come clear. To make sense. I keep waiting. I can't do it any more.

Pace All right. Then tonight we'll run her.

Dalton No. Not tonight.

Pace Tonight.

Dalton That's not what I'm waiting for. It's just a train.

Pace Yeah. Well, it's going somewhere. And it doesn't look back. Tonight, God damn it. You'll run it tonight.

Dalton No. Not me. That was just a game.

Pace We've been working on this for weeks. You can't back down. It's time. I can feel it. Everything's quiet. Everything's waiting. Listen? Hear how quiet it is –

Dalton (*interrupts*) It's just talk, Pace. Just talk. This used to be fun. That's gone. You're gone. I don't know where but you're gone.

Pace I could hurt you. (*She takes out her knife.*)

Dalton I'm not afraid of your knife. You could cut me open but I'd still leave.

Pace jumps him and knocks him down. She sits on him.

Pace What's the matter with you?

Dalton You said you'd change me. You did, God damn it. Now change me back.

Pace I can't.

Dalton Yes you can.

Pace How? Just tell me how.

Dalton I don't know. How the hell am I to know? I didn't do it. You did it. You brought me here. You talked and talked. You put your hands inside my head. You kissed me without kissing me. Tonight. Finally tonight. But not like a girl should. You fucked me but I wasn't even inside you. It's ridiculous. This isn't how I want to be.

Pace How do you want to be?

Dalton Normal. Like any other kid. And satisfied. Like I used to be. Just satisfied. And now. Now I want everything. You did this to me.

Pace Say it.

Dalton No.

Pace Say it.

Dalton No.

Pace I hate you, Pace Creagan.

Dalton Yeah. I do! (*Beat. He's quiet now.*) And there are times I've never been happier; I can't forgive you for that.

Pace touches his face gently, then gets off him. She starts to leave.

Where you going? Pace. Hey. Pace.

She leaves.

*Dalton in his cell, still on his back. Dray enters, quiet
and bewildered. He carries a small pillow. At first,
Dalton tries to ignore him.*

Dalton I was just going to sleep.

Dray Yes. I know it's late.

Dalton Why did you come?

Dray Isn't it natural a father would come?

Dalton You've hardly left the house in months.

Dray holds out the pillow to Dalton.

Dray I brought you your pillow.

Dalton doesn't take it.

Dalton That's not my pillow.

Dray It's not?

Dalton I haven't used it for years. The feathers are
poking out of it. I used to wake up in the night and my
face felt like it was full of nails.

*Dray runs his hand over the pillow. He finds a feather
and pulls it out.*

Dray Yeah. There's one. (*He finds another.*) Here's
another.

*Dray continues to gently comb and search the pillow
and pull out a feather here and a feather there,
sparingly, as the scene continues. Dalton watches this
strangely tender exercise. Dray looks at each feather
he removes, then forgets it as he goes on to another.
The feathers float unnoticed to the ground.*

63

Dalton I don't sleep much in here anyway. (*watching Dray pull the feathers*) So are you going to roast it after you pluck it?

Dray Not as bad as I thought it'd be. Walking the street again.

Dalton It's about time.

Dray 'Course I did have this pillow to hide my face in. You think anyone saw me?

Dalton I hope not.

Dray There's something I want you to do for me.

Dalton You think I killed her.

Dray I want you to touch me.

   Dalton does not respond.

Does the thought. Disgust you?

Dalton You haven't let me. In a long time.

   Dray advances. Dalton is suddenly furious.

Stop right there. Don't, God damn it! (*Beat.*) You think you can come. In here. (*Dalton rips the pillow out of Dray's hands and throws it aside.*) After all this time with this fucking pillow and everything's going to be okay? Yeah. It disgusts me. You disgust me. Like a little fucking kid sitting in your corner week after week waiting for the world to stop. Well it did, Father. At least for me. No. I don't want to touch you. What difference could that make now? To me, you're just a noise in the corner. I won't even notice when you go.

   They are quiet some moments. Dray does not move to leave.

Stay with me.

Dray I don't want to live. Like this.

Dalton How?

Dray Unchanged. Your skin's warm. I can feel it from here. So close to me you smell of. Berries. I don't know. Gasoline. And somewhere behind it all something like, something like. I don't know. I don't – All my life I wanted to say something that mattered. (*Beat.*) I don't know why. (*Beat.*) I've got to get back now. Your mother's gone out. I must. Talk to her. It's getting dark. But the sun's still out. I don't know why. I came.

Dalton To bring me my pillow. (*Beat.*) Go home.

   Dray sits.

Dray Yes. I must get back. At the edge. Not too far. That was our home. What happens when we die?

Dalton How the hell should I know? You should be telling me that. I'm the one who's supposed to die. Christ, what's going on here? They're going to hang me. Do you understand? I told them I killed her.

Dray Did you kill her?

Dalton I don't know.

Dray I think when we die, we just. Disappear. A few handfuls of nothing maybe. And that's it. What do you think?

   Dalton sits down beside him, but not that close.
   Dalton shrugs.

Dalton We just lie down and we don't get back up.

Dray Will it be terrible?

Dalton Some people think there's a light. Some say it comes from above. I don't believe it. If there's anything at all, it'll come up from under the ground. Where we don't expect it. A light. A warm light and it'll cover us.

Dray What colour is the light?

Dalton Who knows?

Dray Red. I think it should be red.

Dalton Yeah. Like the sun, when you look at it with your eyes closed.

After some moments:

I'll touch you now. If you want.

Dray I'm going to close my eyes.

Dalton Why?

Dray So no one will see us.

Dray closes his eyes. Dalton awkwardly rests his head on his father's knee. It is a small gesture. They sit this way together some moments. Then Dalton lifts his head away again. After some moments of silence Dray gets to his feet.

Dalton Wait a minute. I want you to show me how to make a shadow on the wall. Anything. I don't care what.

Dray takes the pillow with him.

Dray It'll take too long.

Dalton I got the time.

Dray (*looking at the small bunch of feathers on the floor*) As though a bird had died here. (*He leaves.*)

Dalton Wait a minute. Wait.

Dalton looks, surprised, at the floor around him. The feathers stir as though a breeze has passed through them.

66

Dray meets Chas as he leaves the cell. They stop and stare at each other. Elsewhere on stage, a feather falls on Dalton, though now Dalton does not seem to notice. A few more fall as the scene progresses.

Chas Never stops talking about you. Thinks you're a hell of a guy.

Dray doesn't respond.

Way a son should. Just like mine.

Dray He's dead.

Chas Looks pretty lively to me.

Dray (*interrupting*) Yours, I mean.

There is an awkward silence.

Chas You're out of work. I've got this job.

Dray Your son was on the track team.

Chas I trained him. Out the old road to the cut-off in Eastwood.

Dray I've got to go.

Chas He says you do shadows.

Dray What of it?

Chas Hey. What's this? Your son never guessed it.

Chas imitates a plane doing a perilous landing. No sound. Dray considers him carefully.

Dray Baby elephant.

Chas Elephant? Like father like son. Wrong, but close. An aeroplane. Motor gone dead. Doing a dead-stick landing. In slow motion of course.

Dray Okay. This?

Dray acts out a camel. With full conviction. Chas circles him, studying Dray's every movement. Dray seems to come alive in this charade, in a way we haven't witnessed before.

Chas Nothing else but a camel, probably a dromedary.

Dray stands stunned.

Dray Yeah.

Chas Not bad at all. Can you do a windmill?

Dray I got to go.

Chas Wait, wait, we just started. I could teach you. I'm teaching your son.

Dray Save it for your own. Goodbye. (*He doesn't move.*)

Chas I'm sort of practising. For him. You know?

Dray You're pretty good.

Chas He was asking for that pillow.

Dray It's not his.

Dray leaves. We hear the sound of someone blowing air. As though they were blowing out matches, but more gently.

SCENE SIX

Pace and Dalton are sitting together, a few feet apart. Pace is blowing on a small feather. We hear the sound of her breath in the silence.
  Then Pace blows the feather into the air, and keeps it above her head, blowing on it, just a little, each time it descends. She lets it land on her upturned face.

Dalton watches this. Pace sees him watching her. She gives him the feather. He tries to copy her. He does so badly. Pace just watches. And laughs. They are enjoying themselves.

Then Dalton 'gets' how to do it. He blows the feather up and keeps it in the air. Paces watches him. Then he lets the feather float slowly down between them.

They are both quietly happy. Because they are no longer alone. Because they are watching each other just being alive.

SCENE SEVEN

Chas is sweeping up the feathers in the cell. Dalton's back is turned.

Chas What do you expect? A hotel or something? There's holes in the roof. Sometimes they build a nest up there. It's the way of the world. They're moving you tomorrow. The trial'll start. It'll be the last of us. Empty cell. Might never get filled, then I'd have to find something else. Move to another jail. Might be no more criminals, not even a rich man who thinks he's a crab. Scuttlin' back and forth. Makes sweeping a devil's job, I can tell you. Still. (*Chas pokes the broom into Dalton's turned back.*) You gonna tell them the truth this time? Only witness was you. Huh, huh? No explanation. No defence. Look, kid. If you talk, if you give them something to make them think you're crazy or sorry or scared, they might not hang you. If you don't talk, they will. Those are the facts.

Dalton doesn't respond. Chas tuts at him.

A nice-faced boy like you. I had a nice-faced boy. (*Chas keeps poking Dalton in the back.*) There was no substance to him. I could knock you down and sweep you up like you were nothing but a scrap of dust.

Suddenly Dalton turns and grabs the broom.

Dalton Hey. Guess what this is?

Dalton slaps himself in the face. Then again. Then he starts to pull his own hair and hit himself, as though someone else is hitting him. He beats himself to the ground in an ugly, violent and awkward manner. Chas watches. Slowly he backs away. They are silent.

Chas I've been good to you.

Dalton Yeah. Brett was a nice boy. He used to hit himself. I saw him do it. Why was he like that? He was a fucking loon, that's why.

Chas Brett wasn't a loon. (*Beat.*) Sometimes. Well. I hit him. In the mornings, right before he went to school. Just about the time he'd start on a bowl of cereal. And a lot of the time, she'd be there. Pace. Your Pace. But I'd hit him anyway. Brett liked her to see it. After I hit him, Brett would take Pace aside and ask her if she saw it. Of course she saw it. She was standing right beside him! But Brett wanted to make sure. Then one morning I'm just about to hit him when he says, 'Wait a minute, Dad. You've got a headache so you just sit back down and take it easy. I'll take care of it.' So Brett hauls off and hits himself in the mouth. And I mean hard. His lip busts and starts bleeding. I'm so surprised that I sit back down and just stare at him. Next morning, the same thing. Brett stands in front of me and hits himself in the face. Twice. I don't say a thing. I just watch. Sometimes him doing it himself, instead of me, made us laugh. Together. The only time we did that. Laugh. (*Beat.*) I knew Brett ran that train. It wasn't the first time. Maybe it was fate.

Dalton It wasn't fate. It was a train. Five hundred and sixty tons of it.

Chas He was. My son. He was waiting. For me to give him something. I couldn't stand it; I didn't have anything to give him. A key to a cell, maybe. A broom to go with it. Is that what you give your child when he grows up? I didn't have anything to give him. So I hit him. I could give him that.

Dalton puts his hands in the feathers. He looks up.

Dalton How do the birds get in? There's no hole in this roof.

Chas What do we do afterwards? I loved him. Years from now?

Dalton What we wanted. It was to live. Just to live.

Chas begins sweeping again. As he sweeps up, he drags the broom across Dalton's hands.

Chas I got to finish up here. Word is there's gonna be trouble down at the plate glass factory. Might be some new guests to replace you any day now.

Dalton About your son. I'm sorry.

Chas Ah. It seems so long ago now; it's all I think about. (*Beat.*) Hey, last chance, kid. Guess what I am? (*Chas sweeps the broom a little wider, almost a figure eight motion, but without much effort.*)

Dalton A giraffe. Grazing. The broom's your neck.

Chas No. Just an old man. Sweeping the floor of his cell.

Dalton stops the broom with his hand.

Dalton Tell them I'm ready to talk.

Chas We're all asleep. It'll have to wait 'til morning. (*Chas leaves.*)

Dalton Hey. I want to talk now. Open the door. Open up the fucking door! I got something to say.

At first he shouts to Chas, who is offstage, then he speaks to himself and finally he is telling us, as though we were the jury, what happened.

Dalton (*shouting*) Pace wanted to make the run that night. I wouldn't do it. I was afraid. No, I was angry.

Pace appears. Dalton doesn't 'see' her but sometimes senses she might be there.

Pace You messed all over my dress!

Dalton (*turning back to his cell door*) But I didn't touch her! I was. Upside down. I was. God damn it –

Pace You don't know what you were.

Dalton I told her to run it alone.

Pace You dared me.

Dalton Pace never could say no to a dare. She stood on the tracks. She was covered in sweat. I stood below the trestle. She looked small up there, near a hundred feet above me. But until she started to run, I never thought she'd do it without me.

Pace I had it made. Bastard. I needed you to watch –

Dalton I could hear her footsteps. Fast, fast –

Pace Because we can't watch ourselves. We can't remember ourselves. Not like we need to.

Dalton Christ, I didn't know she could run like that! She was halfway. She had it crossed. But then I –

Pace Turned around. You just. Did it. (*She 'disappears'.*)

Dalton Then I. Just did it. I turned. Around.

Dalton is propelled into the past moment. Now he can 'see' Pace. But where he looks to see her, high up, we see nothing. The Pace Dalton sees we cannot see,

and the Pace we see is not the Pace Dalton sees.
Elsewhere, we see Pace climbing up the trestle. Dalton
shouts at the Pace we can't see.

Dalton No! No way! I won't be your fucking witness!
You're warped. That's what you are. Everybody says it.
(*Beat.*) Stop. You better stop!

Pace reappears, very high up on what might be a piece
of track. She calls to him.

Pace Dalton. Watch me. Hey! Watch me.

Dalton No. Damn you.

Dalton turns around, so that his back is to both the
Pace we can see and the other Pace we cannot see.

Pace Dalton. Turn around. Watch me.

Dalton is furious and torn as he covers his ears and
shouts.

Dalton God damn you, Pace Creagan! (*Now he is back*
in the present, and he speaks calmly to us. Pace remains
very still on the track.) But I wouldn't turn around. Pace
must've slowed down. And lost her speed, when she was
calling to me. Pace started to run back but she knew
she'd never make it. And then she turned. Even from
where I was at, I could see she was shaking her head.
Back and forth, like she was saying: 'No. No. No.'
(*Beat.*) She didn't want to die.

Pace puts her arms over her head, like she is going to
dive.

Dalton And then she did something funny. Pace couldn't
even swim and there was no water in the creek, but she
was going to dive.

Pace Watch me. Dalton.

Dalton And this time. I watched her.

*This time Dalton turns around, and for the first time
looks at the Pace that we can also see. This time we
all watch Pace.*

*Pace moves as if to dive, there is the tremendous,
deafening roaring of a train that sounds almost like
an explosion, different from the other train sounds we
have heard. Then Pace is 'gone' and we see nothing
more of her. Dalton is 'alone'.*

Pace lay beside the trestle. She wasn't mashed up from
the fall. Only the back of her head. I started to shout at
her. Called her every name I could think of. Even a few
she'd taught me herself. (*Beat.*) And then. And then I did
something. Something I can't. I don't know. It was.
Maybe. It was. Unforgivable: I knelt beside her.

*Dalton stands looking down at the feathers his father
left behind. He is still, quiet, as he speaks.*

Pace never let me kiss her, like that. So I did. And she
didn't try to stop me. How could she? That's what I
can't forget. She once said to me, Dalton, you can't take
anything from me I don't want to give you. But then she
opened her mouth. She was dead. But she opened her
mouth. And I kissed her, the way I'd always wanted to.
And she let me. (*Beat.*) She let me. (*Beat.*) I have to
believe that.

*Dalton swipes the feathers aside. A moment later, we
see Chas again, who lets Dalton out of his jail cell.
We know Dalton is freed.*

Gin appears and watches Dray. Dray is still. Gin is holding in her hands a large piece of glass, which has a small break on one side.

Gin We've swept the place out. Most of the machinery's all right. Glass everywhere. Like hail. We scooped it up. By the bucketful. Three girls from my work are with me. About thirty others. From all over. We threw lots of this out. Thought I'd bring some home. We can use it in the back door. (*calmly*) Put that away.

   Now we see that the shadow Dray is making is a gun. And the gun is not a shadow.

Dray I went to see Dalton. He said at night when he slept, his face was full of nails. All these years. And I didn't know. (*Beat.*) Come here.

Gin I've got to get back to the plant. Are you coming with me?

Dray Just come here.

   Ginny stands by him.

Here.

   He gives her the gun. She just stands there with the gun, hanging at her side, ignoring it.

Gin Almost a shame to sweep up that glass. It was so bright in there. The sun through the windows, hitting the glass on the floor –

Dray (*turns to Ginny and lifts her hand so the gun is at his forehead*) Ginny.

Gin – like we were standing on a lake of ice that was turning to fire right under our feet.

Dray Change me.

Gin does not respond.

Please. Please. Change me.

Gin No. Not like that. (*She puts the gun down between them and moves away.*) Dray. Are you coming with me?

Dray doesn't answer. Dray makes a shadow on the wall. Then another.

Dray What is it? A horse? A dog? I don't know any more.

Gin This is the last time I ask you: are you coming with me?

Dray (*dropping his hands*) Shadows. Just fucking shadows.

Ginny leaves. Dray stands up suddenly, knocking over his chair as he does so. He looks in the direction of Ginny's exit and speaks softly.

Yes. I am.

SCENE NINE

Dalton is in his cell making shadows on the wall, as in the Prologue. Pace appears behind him. They are both in the cell and at the trestle at one and the same time. Pace is dressed in her brother's clothes. She carries her dress. She lays it on the ground and spreads it out carefully.

Pace That's a bird, stupid. A pigeon.

Dalton slowly turns around.

Like the kind that live under the trestle. Haven't you heard them? At dawn they make a racket. (*She's finished laying the dress out. She stands back.*) Lie down on it.

Dalton Why?

Pace Just do it. Or you'll be sorry. Last chance, Chance.

Dalton kneels down on the dress.

Dalton What're you gonna do?

Pace jumps up onto a higher level and turns her back to Dalton. She is exhilarated.

Pace Make something happen!

Dalton Are you going to kick me? Are you mad at me?

Pace Open your shirt.

Dalton What?

Pace Just shut up and do what I tell you. Open your shirt.

Dalton opens his shirt. Throughout their dialogue, Pace never touches herself.

Now. Touch me.

Dalton makes a movement towards her but she cuts him off.

No. Stay still. Right there. And do this. (*Pace puts her own hands near her chest, though she doesn't touch herself.*) Go on.

Dalton copies her.

Right. Now close your eyes. And touch me. It's simple.

Dalton hesitates, then he closes his eyes and touches his own bare chest. Pace is very still, her arms at her side.

Yes. There. You won't hurt me. (*Beat.*) Go on.

Dalton touches his nipples.

That's right. You're touching me. I want you to touch me. (*Pace raises her arms in the air, still facing away from Dalton.*) It's going to happen. To both of us. Go on. Open your legs. (*Beat.*) Do it.

Dalton lies down, and opens his legs.

Now touch me. There. Just touch me.

Dalton touches himself.

Can you feel me? I'm hard.

Dalton moans. He turns over onto his stomach. Pace never looks at him, though she is just as involved as before.

I want to be inside you.

Dalton Pace.

Pace Let me inside you.

Dalton Go on. (*Dalton makes a sharp intake of breath.*)

Pace Does it hurt?

Dalton Yeah.

Pace Good. I can't stop.

Dalton moans again, as though in both pain and pleasure.

Now. Yes. Can you feel me?

Dalton I'll make your dress wet –

Pace Can you feel me?

Dalton Yes.

Pace Where? Tell me. Where can you feel me?

Dalton Inside. Everywhere. Pace. (*Beat.*) You're inside me.

Dalton comes. They are quiet for some moments.

Pace There. We're something else now. You see? (*Only now does Pace turn around.*) We're in another place.

Both of them are quiet and still some moments. Then Dalton opens his eyes. He slowly stands up.
  Pace moves towards the candle. Pace and Dalton do not look at one another.
  Pace crouches over the candle. Dalton makes a slight movement, as though touching his mouth. Then Dalton raises his arms, as though this time welcoming her vision. Pace blows out the candle, at the same moment Dalton seems to do the same. We hear the sound of the candle going out. Then blackout.

End of Play.